Copyright © 2019 by Alice Faye Warren

All rights reserved. This book or any portion thereof
may not be reproduced or used in any manner whatsoever
without the express written permission of the publisher.
Please send such requests to: acmpublish@gmail.com

ISBN: 978-1-7329900-8-1

Printed by: A&C Marketplace Publishing LLP in the
United States of America

INSPIRATIONS FROM GOD

ALICE FAYE WARREN

TABLE OF CONTENTS

Introduction	4
God's Rose	5
Walking	6
A Thought	7
Intimacy	8
God's Garden	9
Husband	10
God's Grace	11
Oh God!	12
Change	13
Expectations	14
The Spirit Attracted Me	15
Praise Him	16
Senses	17
Promise	18
Singleness God's Way	19
God's Love	20
Loving You	21
Butterflies	22
In His Care	23
The Tabernacle	24
Sacrifices	25
Anthology	26
His House	27
A Christmas Prayer	28
The Comforter	29
The Ocean	30
A Birthday Wish	31
Timing	32
Ask! Seek! Knock!	33
God's Love Abounds Around Us	34
Remembrances	35
Excitement	36

INTRODUCTION

Inspirations from God has been a work in progress over several years. When I think back over its genesis, I never dreamed it would come to light in this form. I never envisioned my life as I live it now.

I am still being inspired by the Holy Spirit and on a daily basis I actively read, work and apply the Word to my life.

GOD'S ROSES

My Christian experience has been very unique, in that it happened to me! Yes, I have experienced life from an angle that perhaps a few have had similar events take place, but all woman can identify with.

Being a woman, a Christian woman, to me is like a "Rose". Just picture it in your mind for a brief moment; a bud, tight, restrictive, compact. Each petal representing the many facets of a woman's total existence, caressing each other in the process of opening up, reaching out, and unfolding.

Each petal depending on one another, all being connected but separate yielding, being shaped and molded, continually growing, maturing to full bloom.

Being open to extraneous elements, God being sunshine, rain, earth, fertilizer, all the necessary ingredients for a good root system. Rooted and grounded! Planted solidly and deeply in the Word of God.

The beauty of the rose brings joy and happiness, which denotes strength. The fragrance perfumes the air, leaving scents that linger even though so faint. It's just love!

There is nothing that compares to a rose. Songs, poems, paintings and photographs all attest to this.

God surely loves the rose, all the many varieties and colors. We, as woman, are God's roses going through the stages of budding to full bloom. Some are slow to open. Some open rapidly - depending on variety and environment.

But none being able to bypass any part of the growing process. God, in His wisdom and love, makes it so as I bloom, I can also have the experience of watching others bloom too!

WALKING

The wilderness expresses a Christian walk,
Something that surrounds you, the air, it seems to talk.

The things you see like the colors bursting.
The things you don't see but yet trusting.
Filled with anticipation, excitement,
Rippling through your body.
Knowing that the best is yet to be explored.
Sometimes obstacles block the path.
Or overgrowth of vegetation, conceal the true beauty.

But prayer being the tool, even the weapon,
for remaining barriers.
Even in its vastness,
God has all the creative powers
To give and provide substance.

A THOUGHT

That's what I had been looking for - A vitalization
of one's potentiality!
Some places we search are just that,
A place.

Nothing that gives a refund can consistently stroke or
stimulate your senses in that there is no incentive.

INTIMACY

Your body stretched
So close to mine
Lovingly staring in eyes divine,
A dusky rose-colored haze of light
Touching gently with hands out of sight,
Feeling,
Desire,
Pulsating to a beat,
Climbing steadily to a peak,
Breathless!
It's hard to speak,
Sweet Release!

GOD'S GARDEN

God gathers His flowers, the scents are so sweet,
Arrayed in color, each one unique.
Bluebell, foxglove, all to adorn
Pansy, daffodil - Roses without thorn

Strong and sturdy, standing tall,
Delicate and fragile, yes, some are small.
But, alas, though different,
It takes the same for them all
Water, sunshine breezes that gently blow
Placed in a bouquet, they all seem to glow.

God in His wisdom makes some to vine
And even hang down,
In spite of that, he gives each one petals
That act as a crown.

Shapes, oh, so many - God only knows
But, when we are picked - yes, we are touched.
Thank God it means He loves us, oh, so much.

HUSBANDS

Beautiful faces, up-turned faces
Black, brown, yellow, white and pink.
How many times have you looked at them.
And know just how they think.

Eyes that flash with eager anticipation.
Although insides filled with anger and frustration.
Miracle worker sometimes we attempt to be
Having difficulties — getting Satan to flee.

Kneeling in sweet submission,
Realizing all the conditions.
Bodies that yearn for love, for fulfillment,
Praying for husbands!

GOD'S GRACE

Oh, my daughters, you oughta thank God,
He loves you.

In times of trouble, He's there on the double.
Even though you don't always accept
The way you are, God really cares.

You just need to let Him know
That for Him, you will open the door.
A hedge of thorns all around is prayed
Seems sometimes to be living in a daze.
Depression - Apathy, that's a bitter cup
But, God in His graciousness can lift you up.

OH GOD!

Oh, Lord my God!
I feel the "Love" that thou has given
I know the joy that serving you can bring.
The many blessings that thou has bestowed
Stirs my heart and makes me want to sing.

Oh God!
In all your wondrous Glory
You have the perfect story
Real joy in revealing
Anticipation in believing
Sharing! Receiving!

Oh! The beauty of your graciousness
The bounty of your peacefulness
The magnitude of your Mercy!

CHANGE

Being rearranged,
In God we state our claim
The Holy Spirit will help us maintain
Change!

No more mundane
It's not in vain
You can sustain
Change!

No loss, all gain,
The gift of God we obtain
In His presence remain
The Love of God to retain
Change!

EXPECTATIONS

God in His glory, He don't expect much
Just reach out your hand in return
Yours, He will touch.

He gives us wisdom, freedom, power
Beyond compare,
Use it, He compels us
Use it, if you dare.

Singing praises, we jump and shout
Circumstances arise, we begin to doubt.
Give God a break, He gave one to you.

Just begin to trust in Him,
See what God will do.

THE SPIRIT ATTRACTED ME

Your Love of God keeps my attention,
Knowing the pathway you travel.
Oh! What a joy as I marvel,
A man, a man, a spiritual man.
God's hand in yours so strong He keeps.
Wipes tears from wonderful eyes that weep.
Tall of stature - Slim, yet sleek,
"Messages" Seriousness, Spiritualism,
You daily expound.
"The Love of God"
It's so profound!

PRAISE HIM

Your spirit by your will must pray
Talking to God each and every day
Trusting in Him, come what may.
Obedience to his words he conveys
Guidance He gives, He lights the way
Blessing from above, ahead of me lay
Hallelujah! Hallelujah!
That's what I say!

SENSES

Just a word
It's not absurd,
Just a sound
Smiles instead of frowns,
Just a sign
Thoughts draw you nigh,
Just a thought
Uniqueness is sought,
Just a glance
Feelings of romance.

PROMISE

This Love is written
By someone that is smitten.
I'm hoping for a chance
Real soon, to make romance.

This Love note is sent
I know you understand what is meant.
September is the tentative date
The time is right, let's not hesitate.

SINGLENESS GOD'S WAY

Oh Lord, as I kneel down to pray
Let me experience singleness God's way
Help me to practice right from wrong
Give me strength so I can be strong
In my heart let there be joy
So I can be a bold witness, not shy or coy
Lift my voice in words of praise
Communicating God's way!

Make my hands one that serve
Give me hind feet that are secure
Cleanse me, make my spirit sweet
Being a new creation, that's what I seek
The love of God is what I must convey,
His gentle voice I must obey,
Doing His will each and every day.
Singleness, but God's way!

GOD'S LOVE

The Love of God is sincere,
It will draw you ever near.
There is no reason for you to fear,
His voice so gently can you hear.

The Love of God is divine,
In His presence so sublime
Gently caressing, yes, entwined
External life, what a sign.

The Love of God is steadfast
An eternity that's how long it will last
Heaven expanding, that's how vast
Omnipresent, not a thing of the past.

The Love of God is so profound
It lifts you up when you're down
Spreading the gospel, what a sound
Victory, Power, alas, even a crown.

LOVING YOU

Loving you is special.
Why I really don't know
All I know is what I feel,
It seems somehow to grow.

Loving you is special.
You ask can you be sure
All I know is what I feel,
I know there is no cure.

Loving you is special.
This fact is very clear
All I know is what I feel,
For me you're very dear.

Loving you is special.
Yes, there really is a sign
And I know what I feel.
Into my life you have brought sunshine.

BUTTERFLIES

Graceful, beautiful,
Sunshine Bright,
Breezes gently blowing
Flower arranged contrasting hues,
Fragile, slightly drifting
Butterflies.

What a wonderful playground,
Considering your past,
Can this pleasure last,
Butterflies.

Cocoon, tight restrictive, mummified,
Vulnerable, unattractive
Butterflies.

Wings spread wide,
What a real pleasure to be outside,
Variations in sizes and design,
An ugly duckling turned swan.

IN HIS CARE

Lord, let me stand
In the hollow of your hand.
Lord, your outstretched arms
Protect me from all harm.
Lord, in your sight
Keep me day and night.
Lord, in your heart
Never let me part.
Lord, with every breath
Guide my path.
Lord, when you are near
Teach me to listen so I can hear.
Lord, let me know
Which way I should go.
Lord, let me feel
Your presence when in prayer I kneel!

THE TABERNACLE

The Shekinah Glory shone all about
The presence of God revealed in this, there is no doubt.
A comforter to lead, guide and protect
A new people in Israel to perfect.
Through murmurings and groanings
Instructions to Moses and Aaron for their atoning,
Provisions He made throughout,
Many still continued to doubt.

Korah in rebellion, his life at stake,
Restitution God gave him a chance to make.
God had given a good gift
This, no one can deny,
But just like in days of old, today we continue to cry.

Even now, this day in this very hour,
Satan walks to and fro, to seek who he may devour.
God in the tabernacle, perfect the place
In His presence by His grace
God's Shekinah Glory still shines today.
Enter into his presence, He's still leading the way.

SACRIFICES

No more the bullock
No more the ram
No more the sheep or the turtle dove,
Because the Lamb of God paid for all.

No more rock altars to be built
But, the altar of confession in your heart
No more the burnt offering
No more the meal offering
Only the offering of peace,
Self-sacrifice - that's the offering
God can use.

ANTHOLOGY

Angels, guardians standing close

Nurture, that's what they do most

Thanksgiving to our Father on high

Heavens beyond the clouds in the sky

Obedience, He gently stirs within us

Love and compassion, with these our hearts almost burst

Overcome, the victory is won

God, in Son, He said, well done

You, when yielded to God, you doing.

HIS HOUSE

God said, I'm going to build a house.
In this house, I'm going to build a people
Living stones
To me belong.

God's people, practicing God's principles
In victorious living
Having a death experience
To the things of the world.
A Resurrection experience
To the things of God.

God said, "I'm going to build me a house.
In this house, I'm going to place my people."
Expecting great things from God.

A CHRISTMAS PRAYER

This is a Christmas prayer,
Happiness with you I want to share.
Romance is the object, if you dare.

This is a Christmas Wish.
That you and I together soon can co-exist,
Sharing ideas, nothing will be missed.

This is a Christmas date.
Love for you I don't have to speculate
No question about it, I want to be your roommate.

This could be a Christmas dance,
We don't have to leave it to chance
Prayer or wish, it still points to romance.

THE COMFORTER

The comforter is here, His presence is so near,
Just open up your heart and let Him in
The comforter is here, you do not have to fear
He gives confidence and joy within.

He takes us through tribulation
Then He ministers consolation
In sorrow and despair, the comforter is there.
Acknowledge Him and see Him guide you through.

He gives love so abundantly
Salvation offered freely
To those that believe He'll openly receive
The blessing He wants to give you!

THE OCEAN

As I sit on the ocean front
Lost in my mesmerizing thought
Starring at the stars above
Thanking God for his abundant Love,

The earth's beauty below
The stars brilliant above
Captive by his undying Love
We are His children, and He loves us so.

And every day He lets us know
By the outrageous beauty He shows
Made with His marvelous hands
The trees, the ocean, every grain of sand.

We must open our eyes and see
What there is for you and me
For not to see, you are not aware
A life without God is truly bare!

A BIRTHDAY WISH

I pray that all the desires of your heart be met,
Not only spiritually but physically as well.
May your days be extensive
May you capture the magic
Of complete fulfillment
Desiring those elements that motivate you
To a new awareness of God and self.

TIMING

Lord, sometimes when I move too fast
Forgetting that strength will not last,
When endurance levels are pushed to the max
Like weary notes from a well blown sax,
Flowers picked, the well is dry
Sometimes too tired to even cry,
What does it get you, what does it mean?
Sometimes nothing but a change of scene.

Lord, sometimes when I move too slow,
My way is clouded, which way to go.
Indecision, I'll get to it maybe today
But, don't forget you said that yesterday
Somewhere in between
God in His wisdom, love, and grace
Brings us to rest in that perfect place.

ASK! SEEK! KNOCK!

Question asking is an art
Answering may quell
The seekers anxious inquiry
But they may ask again.

Seek and you shall find
A dimension that was not previously open
Enter in and find rest.

Knock sometimes, it opens doors
Motivating, expanding a creativity of new life.
God's love abounds around us.

GOD'S LOVE ABOUNDS AROUND US

This is a House of Rest
Where prayers are heard, people are blessed.
This is a House of Peace
Where one can be sure God's presence will never cease
And His love is on the increase.

This is a House of Joy
Glad tidings we bring, sweet hosannas ring
Praising a living King.
This a House of Love
Dipped in tranquility emanating from above,
Dripping like rain from God, this is Love.

This is a House of Rest,
Forgiveness, when we confess,
Thanksgiving, when we say, "Yes!"

Compassion He brings,
Prosperity and wealth - These are some of the things.
Strength, power, structure to one's life,
When you're in rest
There is an absence of strife.

This is a House of Rest,
Enter in so you can be blessed

REMEMBRANCES

Thoughts of you are pleasant.
Thoughts of you sometimes create in me an emotion
that is very hard to explain; then why should I explain?

I enjoy remembering the conversations we share.
The responses you give, a sharing of laughter, an idea
transferred, a feeling that permeates the distance and
lingers, even rings in my mind stimulated by certain
words or thought patterns.

Creating images that invoke awareness and motivation,
arousing passions and desires, yet tempered with
patience and growing maturity, blending inner feelings
without word expectation.

Keeping me humble, continually thanking God for the
experience of having our paths cross, thereby enticing,
even tapping, a resource that even I was unaware of but
that I find enlightening.

Joyful, spirit-filled, revealing God's power and blessing.

EXCITEMENT

A - is for ART, it has many different faces
B - is for BRAIN, left and right lobe, simultaneously it paces
C - is for CONSCIOUSNESS or just a thought
D - is for DREAMS which through all is sought
E - is for EYES and EARS, to see through the mind and to hear His voice
F - is for FAITH in which we actively make a choice
G - is for GOD, the Creator of all
H - is for HEALTH in living even before the fall
I - is for the IMAGE of God we all should reflect
J - is the JUDGEMENT if the reflection is incorrect
K - is KONINIA, the Brotherhood of man
L - is the LOVE of God in which we all can stand
M - is the MEMORY subliminally pure
N - is the NEED to know principles to help us endure
O - is OBEDIENCE to the hope of His calling
P - is PRAISE and PRAYER that keeps us from falling
Q - is for QUEST, of the road less traveled, narrow is the way
R - is REVELATION, the truth will convey
S - is for SATAN, the deceiver of the brethren, resist him and he will flee
T - is TRUST and THANKSGIVING in hope of eternity
U - is for UNITY, the gathering as in one
V - is the VICTORY when the conquering is done
W - is for WORSHIP to God, the Lord of our life
X - is for Christ in whom we are healed by His stripes
Y - is for YOU and me in a process of change
Z - is for ZION, the everlasting goal to attain

www.ingramcontent.com/pod-product-compliance
Lightning Source LLC
Chambersburg PA
CBHW051720040426
42446CB00008B/979